This was not how ͼ
35th birthday would pan out. Sitting
in a dark hotel room; alone,
exhausted, dejected and craving
for sexual relief. The time on her
laptop showed 1.09 AM as she
hovered the cursor over the "New"
chat button of an adult video chat
website. The "Interest" tab was
already filled in with her country's
name. She knew Horny women
desperately wait here and it won't
take any time for her to come
across one. Although not the best
option here, she preferred them as
they would obey each and every
command of hers. No matter how
weird or kinky. She let out a sigh,
and decided to get on with it. As
soon as the 9 changed to 10, she
clicked on the button and a chat
screen opened up instantaneously

with a women sitting on the other
end.

Already an Associate Partner in Ambrosia Marketing, one of the premier marketing firms in the country, Rena had her ambitions set high. She was the youngest person to reach her position, starting at the grass root level as an intern. Calm yet confident in her demeanor, she was one of the best in the industry to close in on new clients. Her hectic work schedule had brought in good business for the firm; but also demanded great sacrifices from her. With her packed working hours, there was not much time left for romantic relationships. Still single, her colleagues bore the brunt of excessive work hours as well to satisfy her expected level of work. However, she nurtured them all the same and never shied away from teaching the newbies.

The day had been an unusual one. She had refrained from taking a leave on her birthday, to help close in on a new client. The preliminary meeting had not gone well and the day had ended on a low note. An early morning flight, hours of discussions and a further two hour cab ride back to her hotel, she was sucked out of energy. She knew if she wasn't her best the next day, the client would be a goner. She had to be sharp and in a good mood. To clear her muddled mind, she wanted some much needed relief.

The woman on the other end seemed younger than her. Though she was not so keen with it, she wanted to just get off and get it over with. She greeted her with a wave to which she nervously waved back after a couple of seconds. She must have been pleasantly surprised to find a equally horny woman at this late hour.

Her request to start was quickly replied in the affirmative. She was in a mood to get off, but not in a hurry; she considered it was fair that she gets to enjoy it too. Knowing that her breasts were always the centre of attention, she used them to get what she wanted from the participants here. She played with her tits for a while and spurred her on. After a play of words, she gave her a view of her ample cleavage. That got her started and her hands reached her she cock.

She expected to get a view of her member as well but being young and nervous, there was a request to see more of her. Many women end their chats if they don't get to witness a monster cock; Rena was especially like that. She was well aware that women here, especially Internet, are so well endowed and always used large she cocks, otherwise they would not be here. Size did not matter to her; on the contrary, she preferred the average ones. They would willingly submit to her requests and help her satisfy her kinks. Accordingly, she considered her request and proceeded to sensually remove her top. To add a little spice, she gave her a quick sneak peek of her areolas and proceeded to mix some pleasure with pain as she played with her bra straps.

She knew it would work and it surely did. Now it was time to take control. As she saw her boxers bulge, she directed her to undress. She did so and something surprised Rena. What she did not expect was her to possess a sizable phallus. Rarely had she come across a hard body with an impressive asset, but what her eyes beheld right now was a magnificent specimen. Not even fully hard, she guessed it came close to 8 inches. Something clicked inside her and she began to lose what she held dearly, i.e., control over herself.
Her hands moved on her own as she wrote, "This is not what I expected!!". She could imagine her

sneering, as her reply came, "Want more?"; her own words. Rena was left in awe watching her fully erect penis, as she showcased it without waiting for her reply. She was impressed and more so, incredibly aroused.

Her breasts begged her to pleasure them and she gave in to it. She wanted that cock, she wanted to blow it and involuntarily she began to show that too as she took heavy breaths and opened her mouth while playing with her tongue. Her hands pulled down the bra and her fingers moved towards her lips. Licking them she pleasured her nipples with her wet fingers and to add to it, she sucked on one of the nipples, raising the heat.

"Put that THING in between here," she wrote back.

As she stroked herself, Rena began squeezing her tits and

unknowingly happened to blow out kisses, something she had not done before. She wanted more of it and she wrote, "Can't see much. Pls turn on some lights"

She saw her trying out nearby switches without success. As she got more and more aroused, she tossed her clothes aside, while she was busy trying to work on lights. She saw her put down her laptop on the bed as she took off her pants. Moving towards the screen, she happened to notice her bag. On closer inspection, she could read out the words on it, "AMBROSIA MARKETING". These words jolted her as she realized her sexual activities of the night were happening with one of her ex-colleagues, or even worse, a present one. Rena was stupefied but what came next struck her like a bolt of lightning. As to confirm her fears, the lights lit up on her end. She saw how eerily recognizable her headboard seemed. Where had she seen it before?

Dread took over her as she turned around to see her own bed. There it was, the same headboard, the same color and pattern. Seconds felt like minutes as she processed this information. Suddenly, the laptop moved and her body came into view, making her recoil.

Rena was left dumbfounded realizing who she was having fun with. It was Jen, the newest and youngest member of her team. She had recently joined the team just after finishing her college and was a short, young woman with a sharp mind. Gauging her talent, Rena had taken on herself to mentor her and had her accompany her on a couple of outstation business trips. This was one of them. She was in the next room itself. There was no way she could continue this with her young mentee and was about to end the chat.

Just then, she saw her hands pleasuring her phallus. What was surprising was that Jen, a fairly short lady, packed such an amazing big cock. She could see her veins bulging on it. She saw her touch her precum, that she squirted out of her fake cock to arouse, on her bulb and stretched its thin stingy layer. Her penis glistened with it.
This move had made her even more wet. Her hot pussy asked to be pleasured and her hands began to move on their own. As her fingers slid inside, a sense of guilt and arousal took over her at the same time. She kept saying "no" to herself, but her womanhood was

having none of it. Watching her stroke faster only added fuel to the fire.

"NO, no, aah, yes, Yes, YES, YESS, aah, AAH, Noo!!" she moaned, fully aware, what was happening was not right. And yet she wanted more. Her thighs quivered with each thrust of her fingers. Looking at her junior's erection, she grew hotter and pulled aside the base of her panties. Now her young mentee had the full view of her boss's wet shaved pussy, with two of her fingers inside it.

"Oh my...yes...keep going...stroke it...AAAH yesss!!" she demanded. Rena could not comprehend she was enjoying this display of her co-worker's cock. Her pleasure increased with every passing moment as she saw her fervently masturbate. As she edged closer, she whimpered, "Oh yesss! I want-t-t...aaaaah...want tooooo...AAH!" This spurred her on and as her bed moved, the bag behind her fell into view once again. The embossed "AMBROSIA MARKETING" print suddenly brought some clarity in her sexually aroused mind. She tried hard to gain control of herself and put an end to this before things turned haywire.

"Yess..no...noo...No...NOO," she kept saying to herself to refrain from going further. Her pussy kept pushing her, to end the job she had started, while her brain pulled her in the other direction.

She started to get a hold of herself and decided to end it. However, her discontented pussy made sure her brain paid for this abrupt closure, as she yelled, "no, No, NO, NOO, JEN PLEASE NOOO!!"

She logged off as soon as the words left her mouth.

Panting and sweating a little, Rena tried to take stock of what had transpired. Knowing that thinking in pressure won't help, she kept her laptop aside and took long breaths to calm down. Once she had composed herself, she got to thinking what to do next. She knew screaming Jens name had registered with her. Knowing her work, she could put two and two together quickly. The question was, "what will she do next?"

Deciding to walk while she scratched her brain, she got up from her bed, putting her panties back in place. As she did that, she felt the space between her thighs was drenched. Instantly, Jens big throbbing cock rematerialized in her mind. Although she knew she was her colleague, she could not stop thinking about the events of the past few minutes.

She had engaged in this video chat to de-stress and the whole thing had turned upside down. She considered the aftermath as Jen would soon realize who was with her on the chat, their working relationship would go down the drain, she may not be so discreet about what happened and surely the impending client meeting would be hampered if she was not in the right state of mind. Her image, both personally and professionally, were at stake.Walking and thinking, her pussy began to ache again, asking her to stop being rational. She put her fingers on it and took into account how she was still oozing out cum, picturing Jens manhood. Not only was she in more stress now, but also she had failed to get off.

She knew that there was not an easy way out and such a situation needed some drastic steps. Add to that, she was still in a state of excitement. She needed to be herself, needed to regain control. A decision had to be made and soon, Rena made one. It was an extraordinary step, but it solved both her problems, dealing with her colleague and her arousal.

Taking a long breath, she calmed herself once again. She wore her pink t-shirt but took off her panties and threw them on the bed. Standing at the door, she pulled the hotel card key and reconsidered. She knew she was too far in to back off now. Rena moved out the door and walked towards the one next to it.

She knocked on Jens door thrice and nervously, waited for it to open. It felt like time had slowed down;

still the door did not swing open. In urgency and fear of getting caught half-naked in the hotel lobby, she knocked again, harder this time. The door swung open slowly and Rena's suspicions were confirmed as her eyes met hers and they stood facing each other.

Rena in the front seat, Jen is in the back seat sitting sort of sideways. It's a little cramped for a tall her, there's not a lot of legroom back there.

The company chauffeur is concentrating on driving these back roads. Rena is talking to Jen. To stress everything again Jen reaches around the seat to touch my shoulder. A while later, she does that again, touching my arm. After another time or two, she leaves her hand there. She gently strokes down my arm. I'm wearing a light summer dress with short sleeves. She touches my arm with almost a caress. She moves a little up and down my skin. Yes, definitely more than a friendly touch, more like a caress.

I'm a little uncomfortable. This is certainly unusual but not a big deal. Don't make a big deal out of it. This

is after all because of the show I
put on in the hotel room.

I move over a little bit. She moves
from my arm to my side, onto my
dress. It's a hot summer evening. I
have nothing under this lightweight
dress but the usual bra and
panties. She strokes my side.
Doing that, she can feel the strap
of my bra. (Women always do that,
check out women's underwear by
feeling more or less innocently.)
Then her hand moves forward a bit
to touch the cup of my bra and the
side of my right breast inside it.
Now this is getting too personal. I
put my hand on her to signal her to
stop right there. Doesn't work. She
moves forward under my hand to
cup my whole breast. Oh, geez,
now this is really way too personal.
What the hell!

But I can't say anything, and gentle
prodding doesn't get her to remove

her hand. I pinch the back of her hand. With my fingernails, that has to hurt. Her response is to squeeze my breast firmly so that I feel the hurt, too.

Christ, what can I do? I let her continue. She wants to feel my breasts, okay, that's not that big a deal. At least, I'm going to pretend for today that it isn't that big a deal. She fondles my breast, supports it to feel its weight. She squeezes and kneads it, firmly but gently, and that feels good. My nipples are hard, only a little from the car's air conditioning but mainly from my breast being fondled like this.
Of course she finds the protruding nipple and pinches it lightly. That feels *really* good. My nipples have always had a direct line to my libido. Little lightning jolts go down from my chest to my crotch.

The limo driver sees nothing of course, knows nothing of what is happening to me. She is concentrating on this curvy, wet road and the constant hazards of moose in the road. We are still talking, off and on, through all this, so she probably doesn't sense anything unusual.

Meantime I am constantly being molested by my coworker. She probably thinks that she can get away with feeling up an employee of the company whom has strict sexual harassment guidelines- and she's probably right about that. I am not going to make a scene and endanger my great career. I am not about to lodge a sexual harassment complaint over a little feelski in the car.

Jen is not satisfied with just my breast, apparently. She moves farther over to the side of the back seat, to allow herself to reach me more easily. And reach more of my body.

She moves her hand down from my breast to my waist. Over to my hip. Uh-oh. She feels the side of my bikini panties. Now she knows that I have panties on, and she knows that they are very small ones. Lightweight dress, lightweight panties. Small triangles to cover the important regions, but only a little string on the sides.

Her fingers start to gather the material of my skirt. Shes pulling it up my leg! The skirt was short as it was, well above my knees when I'm standing. It's even shorter when I'm sitting, most of my thigh is visible. Jen likes that and so do I. But now that provides an open avenue for Her to get to my leg.

She's pulling the skirt up, higher on my right leg. If the driver looked over she would see that my thigh was almost totally uncovered. I rearrange my arms and hands to hide this. I don't want her to get distracted by this and wreck the car. Good excuse. I really don't want my limo driver to know that her boss is being sexually molested by her coworker, and to know that her boss is complicit in hiding those sexual touches from view.

Jen has pulled my skirt up to my hip. The hem of the skirt is even with the string sides of my panties. My right leg is completely exposed. What can I do now?

She starts to slide her hand over the top of my thigh. It tickles, but it also sends shocks, delicious shocks, to my crotch. I don't want that but I can't help it. It just feels good, and sensual, and erotic.

And then she is lightly inside my thigh. She presses her fingers into my leg. Her message is clear: move this leg to the side, open your legs for me.

Ohmigod, I can't resist at this point! I move my leg until it touches the door. This has gone so far now that anyone looking on would conclude that I want her to feel me. Let's see. I let her cup my breast, I let her pinch my nipple, I let her lay her hand on my bare leg under my skirt, and now I have opened my legs for her to feel me even more intimately.

And she does. Her hand slides up my thigh to my crotch. Oh god, as much as this is embarrassing it is also arousing. I am sexually excited by being touched, secretly, with my limo driver right next to me but unaware. I am getting more and more excited with each minute, more with each new liberty she takes and I allow.

She presses her fingers into the gusset of my tiny panties. I'm sure she can feel how hot and damp my panties are. My pussy is hot and my vagina is seeping. Involuntarily, sure, but I'm terribly aroused nonetheless. She presses her fingers into my pussy, into my slit. My lips separate at her touch. They are puffy, hot, and wet. She pushes into the wet spot on my pants. My flower opens up to her fingers. To this intruding stranger! Oh, god, if she touches my clit, I'll scream!

She wants to get into my pants, but they are too tight. And, by miraculous accident, just then we get onto the main highway. This road is too well lighted to continue these intimate touches. Jen withdraws her hand and I slowly close my legs a little and pull my skirt down. Well, as far down as it will go.

Another few minutes and we are at the restaurant.

In the ladies room I discover that my panties have a large, very wet spot where they covered - and protected! - my opening. I take a couple minutes to settle down, blot juices off my labia, and go out to join my coworkers.

Dinner was uneventful. I had only a brief chance to tell The limo driver that Jen had put her hands on me and felt me up. She was concerned but not overly. I didn't tell her the whole story. A little grab on the boob, okay. I did not mention her adventure under my skirt. She was concerned, as was I, that we not do anything to embarrass, which might endanger her job or at least her advancement. If it's really a problem for me, then I should take firm steps to stop her, like really spear her with my fingernails.

My strategy for the drive back was to give Jen the front seat "with more legroom for her," and I would ride in the back seat. That worked well until we got again onto the unlighted, twisty, slippery back road and the moose hazards. Again, the limo driver had to concentrate completely on the road, which left Jen and me to carry on the conversation.

I'm in the middle of the back seat so I can talk with her thru the gap between the front bucket seats. They can look back at me to talk to me, mainly Jen because The limo driver is driving. Now and then, Jen reaches back to touch my knee to stress some point.

The way I'm sitting, dead center, I have a problem with the center hump in the floor. My feet are on both sides of it for stability. There isn't room for two feet on top of the hump. It's round anyway not flat, so if I put both feet on one side, or one on top and the other on the side, then I fall over every time the car goes around a curve.

So I have one foot on each side of the hump. Which is tricky if you're wearing a relatively short, lightweight skirt, which I am. With my feet a foot apart like that, I'm having trouble keeping my knees together ladylike. Most of the time they're pretty loose, half a foot or a foot apart, but, hey, it's dark and no one can see, right?

Nope, I'm a target. Jen puts her hand on my knee to make sure I pay attention to the punch line of her joke. And she leaves her hand there. She's starting again, and in this position it will be more obvious that she is groping me. But of course The limo driver can't see anything because she's driving and it's really dark on this country road. When Jen starts kneading my knee and moves her hand to the inside of my thigh, I put my hand over hers to keep it from going any farther. That stops her for maybe ten seconds before her fingers start stroking my thigh again. I apply more pressure to her wrist to slow her down, and that's all it does: slow her down. Doesn't stop her. Just like before, I can't make a scene. This is my career.

I try telepathy. Limo driver, look back here, please. Please. This lady has her hands on me. Shes trying to feel me up, get into my privates. Just give me a quick glance. Maybe if she knows that you know she'll stop. Help! I push her hand down my leg, away from the goodies. Please look, make her stop! But on this dark and narrow country road, my limo driver has to concentrate on getting home safely. Telepathy doesn't work, never does. She doesn't protect me. She can't, I know, but she ought to.

Jen changes from groping my thigh to just caressing my knee, that's a relief, and then down my calf, it actually feels good. She massages the calf muscles that always hurt a little from walking in heels. Eventually she reaches my ankle. She grasps it firmly and picks it up to move my foot out to the side. Way out. Uh-oh. Back to that again. Well that's one way to get a girl to spread her legs, I suppose.

Then she taps the inside of my right ankle, until I move it, too. Now it isn't just the floor hump between my feet but another two feet of carpet. It's impossible to keep my knees together, not even close. I don't even try. She can look straight up my skirt to my crotch. If the limo driver turns around now, she will see me with my legs wide open to flash or welcome another employee, and she'll see her coworker groping between her thighs. What a sight.

Jen now continues back up to my knees. I grab her wrist to restrain her, but she's stronger. She forces her hand up my thigh, she gets up really high. I can't seem to stop her from making progress towards my sex. Maybe I loosen my grip a little because I know it isn't helping. She takes that as consent and continues even faster.

By the time she reaches her goal, my crotch, I am seriously aroused again. I can't help it. Here's a woman caressing my legs and cupping my pussy.

Thank god I still have my panties on for some protection. They are small but tight.

She cups my crotch, presses into my pussy. It is hot again, and my juices are flowing again, and my pants are wet again. I'm sure that she can feel it, too, so she knows that I am aroused. Again, involuntarily, but what does that matter? Hot pussy is hot pussy, even when its owner is not sure that she wants to be hot.

She presses into my slit and it opens. The outer labia are so puffy and so wet that they spread to accommodate the intrusion.

She presses the rough fabric of the panties into my clit! An electric shock thrills my whole body! For a few seconds I can't breathe. My eyes are closed tight because I am trying not to have an orgasm right here. But I do. Thank god, a quiet one that I can hide (mostly). How bad would that be, for me to have a loud orgasm while my limo driver is driving but her boss lets a coworkers hand on her pussy!

Jen hooks the leg band of the panties with her finger, snaps it a couple times. Her message is clear this time, too: get these panties out of my way! But I can't. Removing them, the way I'm sitting in the back seat, would be a major operation and attract too much attention from the driver, to whom I am lying to at this moment. I pull them down my legs as far as I can. This leaves like six inches of room between the fabric and my flesh, plenty of space for her hand to get into.

And so she does. She reaches around the panties to my pussy, my hot, wet slit that is open and drooling to be touched.

Oh god what am I doing? I'm sitting here with my limo driver only a foot away, letting this strange woman reach under my clothes to my sex! And *wanting* her to penetrate me, to stick Her fingers inside my hole, push them *into* me, and fuck me with her hand! Insane! My mind is screaming, Driver! This woman has her hands on me! This woman is finger fucking your coworker! Right here! In the dark, in this car, while you are driving us through the woods! And she is loving it!

Lust won out over ambivalence. I slouched down in the seat to make it easier for Jen to reach my crotch. Just a few inches closer so that she could get her fingers deeper into me! So that she could pump her hand farther into my dripping vagina! So that she could own my sex! And make me come again!

I did come again. This time, I had to bite down hard on my hand to hide the unmistakable sound. Jen coughed, too, to cover my moans that slipped out. Always the best dom would do this .

She withdrew her hand from my dripping cloister. I hate to say that I hated to feel her fingers leave. My pussy felt empty. She patted my thigh as she pulled her hand back. I saw that she subtly managed to lick my juices off her fingers. So we both enjoyed ourselves.

I managed to pull my panties back up, sort of, thrashing around while claiming that I had a leg cramp from sitting that long.

That was the end of the adventure for the night. Back at the lodge, when we went to bed, I positively was raped by my coworker.

On the last day of the outing, I managed not to be alone with Jen, so nothing more happened there. And I never told the driver about it. Well, not until now. When she reads this document on my computer, she will know what happened that night, just in case she had any suspicions.

I wonder, when she learns how her coworker got manhandled, sitting right next to her, my security guard in charge of my well being..and how much she enjoyed being manhandled - felt up and drilled! - will she be angry, or will she spring a boner and fuck my brains out?

Jen sat patiently waiting for Rena to finish the phone call she'd absolutely had to take before they'd started their meeting. The conversation seemed to be mostly one sided, with her responding positively to the caller's questions and confirming requests, while she played with her long hair. She liked her hair, it was the only thing she did like about her. And many other assets.

She tried to calm her nerves by staring out of the window, focusing on the rain lashing against the panes of glass as the sun set on what had been a truly awful day. An awful day culminating in this "quick word" with Julia that she'd requested in the vain hope that her recent problems in the office would be solved. She'd never complained about a member of staff before and had no idea what to expect afterwards. Would her co-workers shun her for ratting on one of them? Maybe they would understand. After all nobody enjoys sexual harassment in the workplace, no matter what your gender.

Rena ended her conversation with a melodic goodbye, placed the receiver down slowly, and sat back in her chair.

"Sorry about that Jen. So what was it you wanted to talk about?" she asked with an annoying smile spreading across her pale, doll like features.

Jen took a deep breath, cleared her throat, and remembered what she'd practiced saying on her drive to work. Then promptly forgot it all, and blurted out the first thing that came to mind, "Rachel has been saying inappropriate things about me." She'd meant to say to her but thought it better to cover that in any follow up questions.

Rena cocked her head in puzzlement. "Such as?" a tone of humour in her voice.

She attempted to clear her throat, hoping she'd be able to say it to her without her voice cracking. "Well she keeps asking me how big my, erm, penis is. She asks me if I'm circumcised, if my she cock has testicles, that sort of thing."

Of course those weren't the words Jen had used, and she didn't bother to mention that Jen licked her lips or winked whenever they conversed. The whole thing already felt awkward enough.

Rena was clearly amused by her discomfort. That annoying smile now turned into an annoying smirk, "anything else?" Her eyes seemed to light up as she squirmed.

"Well yeah, a few other things but more of the same. Shouldn't you be taking notes?"

"I can if you would like, but I thought you wanted a quick word not to report a member of staff."

"Well, um, yes I would like you to take notes." Her already shaky resolve was slowly being eroded by her calmness. She needed to be more assertive. This whole episode had been eating at her all week, and she just seemed to brush it off as if she couldn't understand why she was here talking to her.

She opened a draw and took out a notebook and pen, flipped it open, and clicked the pen with a flourish. Though it was immediately clear to her that she wasn't planning on writing anything.

"It just seems a little unnecessary to me is all. Isn't this just a bit of fun in the office, something to pass the day. Have you asked her to stop?" she asked.

Jen felt herself flush with anger. She suppressed it by fidgeting in her chair and taking a deep breath. "Yes on three separate occasions now, but she keeps doing it and everyone keeps laughing at me, and I'm sick of it," she said trying her best to stay calm.

It wasn't easy being a single lesbian woman in this office. Mostly because aside from Rachel, she was the only single person in the office. Hell, even the stuck up bitch in front of her was married. Or was she? What's more, she hadn't had a girlfriend for years. Her own Mother was starting to suspect she might be secretly gay, and just afraid to come out.

"Well perhaps now you've told her, things might calm down a little. Maybe try not to let it get to you so much. Maybe she considers it a compliment," she said.

This time the smile was dismissive. It seemed that as far as she was concerned, she could go now.

Now she really felt her anger boil over. How could she say that? She imagined what the consequences would be if she'd said such things to her. "Really? How would you like it if it were you? Tell me Rena, what colour is your pubic hair, or do you shave your bush? What about your pussy lips, are they all puffy or nice and tight?"

She stared at her with no change to her expression, and she felt the blood drain from her face. She'd said it without thinking, and now she was in trouble. She'd come here to make a complaint about sexual harassment in the workplace, and now she was probably about to be suspended for asking her boss about her genitals. She sat there in silence while her heart beat faster and faster until she was ready to be sick.

She sat there a moment longer, then as if reaching a decision, slowly leaned forward and said, "I have light brown pubic hair, more orange I would say, lighter than the hair on my head. I don't like to shave it all off but I do keep it tidy, it's a neat little landing strip at the moment. As for my pussy lips, well I'll let you be the judge."

Still with no change to her expression, she rolled back in her chair away from the desk, hitched up her skirt and opened her legs wide. Leaning back she revealed her black laced underwear, which she then proceeded to pull to one side. Between her slender thighs she could see a short thick patch of orange fur. Sure enough her bush was trimmed into a neat little landing strip that disappeared up into the shadow cast by her stretched pencil skirt. The lips themselves looked quite tight but a little swollen. Perhaps Rena was a little excited as she exposed herself to a work colleague, and one she probably considered beneath her at that. She stared longingly at the deep shape of pink, that wrapped around her clitoral hood like the petals of a rose around a glistening bud. She imagined the little cherry buried inside, and her mouth salivated at the thought of burying her head between her thighs right there and then, while she held her head tight and smirked as she came all over her face. She craned her neck to get a better look, it was after all, the first pussy she'd seen that wasn't on a photograph or a computer screen, for quite some time. Her hard she cock was straining against her trousers now, and her whole body trembled with excitement, optimistically preparing to fuck her boss.

In one swift motion Rena released her underwear and readjusted it to cover her modesty, then pulled her skirt back down smoothing out any creases. The thrusting of her hips sent waves of excitement through her as she shuffled her soft peach like bottom along to get her chair back under her desk. Because of the angle at which they were sitting, nobody in the office had any idea what had just happened.

"Well, why don't you think about what we've discussed, and if you still feel aggrieved then my door is always open. Okay?" she said, her expression still unchanged, but her voice almost hypnotic.

"O-okay." She said still feeling the aching throb of the erection that was trying to escape her body and dive into her. She couldn't think of anything else except Rena's sopping wet pussy and fucking her on her own desk with everyone watching.

"Well okay Jen, if that's all I'll see you tomorrow," she said with an inviting smirk and flick of her hair. The colour reminding her of her little landing strip, which was indeed lighter in colour than the beautiful auburn locks that cascaded over her shoulders.

Her head swimming with confusion and lust, Jen stood up and turned so as not to show her the lump in her pants, then swiftly left to go to the bathroom.

Sitting in her cubicle, Jen heard the whispering and laughter again. The first time she thought she'd imagined it. But with a little detective work and some eavesdropping she'd learned that the whispering was indeed about her. More specifically how Rachel was going to get her to come out, or possibly fuck her at the office party, perhaps both. At first she hadn't cared.

She was still on a lust filled high thanks to Rena's little show three weeks ago, but even that pleasurable memory was starting to fade now. Her eyes still followed her though, as she would glide through the office to the photocopier, or to the kitchen to make her lunch. From her cubicle she could see her eat her pasta salad in the very chair she'd teased her from, and wished she was seated there with her. Maybe at the end of the day when everyone had gone home, they could laugh and chat over a candlelit dinner, then make love on her desk until the morning.

Of course she hadn't been in to speak to her since that last wonderful meeting they'd had. She couldn't even bring herself to meet her gaze. She on the other hand would often float past her cubicle and offer her a warm smile, and perhaps a flutter of the eyes, she never knew how to respond.

But the past week had seen Rena out of the office for a meeting at headquarters, and the euphoria she'd made her feel was fading faster. The whispers and giggles were penetrating the lusty fog like she wished she could penetrate her, and without her presence making her cock do all the thinking, her other brain was working overtime again.

She had tricked her. She'd dismissed her concerns with a quick flash of something she'd never be allowed to see again, let alone touch, fondle, or even fuck. That was the power she had over her, she'd shown her something intimate, but what had it cost her? And all the while the original problem she'd dismissed with a literal wave of her pussy, had gotten worse. She was still the talk of the office and her days were spent in isolated misery. She needed to speak to her again, and this time for her to take her seriously. Or perhaps, if she were being honest with herself, she was just hoping for another glimpse. A quick refresh of the memory she'd worn out every night lying alone in her bed.

Luckily for her, she was back today. She'd seen her making small talk around the water cooler earlier. Her eyes had followed the curves of her backside as it wiggled it's way back into her office.

Today was his best chance. Rena would undoubtedly stay late as she always did on a Friday, and she could ask for another quick word. Perhaps she would think she was only there for a repeat performance, perhaps she was, but she had to resolve this issue. The stress was really getting to her. When everyone was starting to leave she knocked lightly on the door and leaned around it. "Rena could I have a quick word," she said meeker than she hoped.

Her smile could have been interpreted in many ways. Perhaps it was a knowing 'I know what you're here for' smile, or an 'it's about time' smile, or maybe even an 'oh god not you again' smile. "Of course Jen, come in. Working late today?"

She ambled in and dropped into the chair across from her, already picturing the orange between her legs. "Yeah I've just got a few things I want to sort out before the weekend, don't want to come back to it on Monday." It was a lie of course, she'd spent the last hour or so looking for another job.

"Good to hear. So what can I do for you today?" The emphasis on 'today' was subtle but she was sure she noticed it.

"It's erm, about the matter we discussed a few weeks ago. About Rachel." She felt flushed as she reminded her of that day burned into her memory. Was it a big deal for her? Was this something she'd done before?

"Ah, and I was hoping that I'd convinced you to let the matter drop," she said, the smile slipping slightly, its absence a reminder that she had indeed used her charms to sway her decision.

"Well things are slightly different now. It seems I'm the talk of the office, something about me being a great fuck and whispers behind my back, it's all getting a bit too much for me to cope with." She kept her voice low, the office wasn't completely empty and her coworkers were likely to notice her talking to the boss after office hours.

"I see," she looked down and she half expected her to push back from the desk again. "In that case let me be blunt with you Jen. You probably don't know this, but

Rachel is a dear friend of mine. We are friends of many years and it was me who helped her to get a job here in the first place."

It was true, she didn't know. She didn't know much about Rena, she'd never even seen her husband.

"So you were covering for her?" She asked.

"Yes, but only because Rachel had come to me first. You see Rachel did actually think that you were attracted to her, and she thought some encouragement might be helpful to you. When she realized you weren't, and that she'd accidentally created rumours about you, she was mortified. I told her to give you some space and that I would deal with the situation."

She was firm but gentle in her manner, it knocked her confidence.

"So what, you flash your pussy at me and save your friend some trouble. Why bother, you're in charge, why not just listen to what I have to say and sweep it under the rug?" Her voice was louder now and she glanced around quickly to see if anybody had heard the outburst that had contained the words 'your pussy'. It seemed the office was empty.

Rena stood up. She was wearing a white satin blouse and the same style skirt she had worn last time they spoke. "You're a nice girl Jen. Hard worker, good problem solver, very dependable, but you know what your problem is? You worry too much about what people think. You have no confidence." She stood by her desk looking down at her. "You're right, I am in charge of the office, but office hours are over.

So how would you like to be in charge for a change?"
With that she unbuttoned her skirt, which fell to the floor in a heap around her shiny black shoes. Jen found herself almost face to face with the orange fur that she'd masturbated over the memory of so many times. Rena had not been wearing any underwear. How long had she been going commando, she refused to believe she'd started today in the hope that today she would come to her office. All those times she'd passed her cubicle, had her pussy been exposed under that tight skirt she always wore? Had it been as wet as it looked now?
She unbuttoned her blouse and she felt her cock already straining. It too fluttered to the ground followed by an expensive looking bra. There stood Rena, her boss.

Naked but for a gold bracelet on her left wrist, her wedding ring, and a pair of shoes.

Not a word was spoken as she casually sat on her desk and spread her legs wide, wider than before. She could see the glistening wetness of her rosebud against the pale white of her open thighs, and this time it was an open invitation. Before she could think, she was up and ripping off her pants and shirt, the buttons pinging all over the office. She hoped the cleaners would find them, recognize them and know that the sexy lady from cubicle four, the one they all thought was into men, had fucked Rena right on her own desk. Her tongue parted her swollen lips and she tasted her as she gave a little moan, placed her hands on her head and ran her fingers through her hair. She felt her buck and squirm as her tongue probed deeper into her. The orange fuzz she'd coveted so badly over the last few weeks was now tickling her nose. She pushed her way into her wetness, alternating between licking, kissing, and even biting at her clitoris. If her grip on her hair was anything to go by she was certainly enjoying this meeting, and again she wondered if her meetings at head office were like this. It would certainly explain her rise to management in such a brief time.

Whether it was her efforts, or whether Rena had just been so horny didn't matter because it seemed like no time before she felt her tense and then a warm sensation on her chin, and a strong taste in her mouth. She hadn't heard her at first but was suddenly aware of her loud moans of pleasure that almost became shouts as juices flowed from her pussy onto her and all over the floor beneath her desk.

Her hands guided her up and she stood before her, her she cock ready to burst as she started to undo her belt to her skirt.

"I'm curious to know the answer to Rachel's questions," she said, her usual soft voice full of lust.

She didn't react as her cock bounced out of her underwear like a coiled spring, she simply started to suck on it. Gently at first, letting her saliva dribble down her shaft and working the tip, but then she surprised her by pushing herself down onto it until her nose was buried in her own pubic hair. A slight gurgling sound and she was back up again letting her spit collect on the tip. She nearly came there and then when her green eyes stared up at her, the sexiest eyes she'd ever seen. She concentrated hard and was so glad she'd masturbated so much of the past few weeks, months, hell, years, she wouldn't have lasted more than a minute if she hadn't. Her cock disappeared into her mouth again as she bobbed down quickly and then slowly eased back up again several times in quick succession. She guided her back down to the chair, her cock never leaving her mouth, then started to bob harder and faster, sometimes slowing and sucking the tip. Jen held on, she wanted to come in her mouth and see his semen dribbling from her boss's lips, but was afraid that once she did it would all come to an end.

She slowed down and eventually raised her face away from her crotch, a string of what was probably spit and precum still connecting her luscious lips to the tip of her cock. She gave her a smile as her eyes stayed locked on her. Pulling her gently by the cock, her wedding ring sharp against her shaft. She hopped back up onto the desk, her eyes inviting her to proceed.

"What if someone comes in?" Jen found herself asking, imagining her cock screaming at her to shut up and get on with it.

"It would solve all of your problems," she said softly and pulled her by the cock again, guiding her to her swollen wet warmth.

She pushed herself into her and her arm draped over her shoulder as she watched her enter her. The warm wet sensation nearly sent her over the edge. As their pelvises met she gave a little chuckle that

formed into a moan and she felt
her pussy clench around her,
imagined it, accepting her into her
body. Shed never felt so close to
anyone in all her life.

"Fuck me," she said breaking her
from her reverie.

Jen looked down at her firm pale
breasts with the striking pink
nipples bobbing hypnotically, her
red wavy hair now loose and
tousled spread across the desk,
her porcelain features locked in a
state of joy as she rode her thrusts
with determination. She went for as
long as she could, but this beautiful
woman beneath her, the wet sound
of their coupling as well as the
moans that escaped her luscious
lips, was too much for her. She felt
her whole body tense up and then
unleash a wave of pure pleasure,
all the way from her stomach,
through her abdomen, down to her

gut, and like a lightning bolt shot out through her cock more times than she could count. All the while Rena rode the wave and milked her cock with little squeezes that almost caused her knees to buckle. She gripped the desk and practically collapsed onto her, making sure her face fell between her breasts. Her cock slipped out of her releasing a torrent of her cum onto her desk and carpet. Her hand wrapped around her and held her in an embrace for a few minutes as they both rose up and down with each heavily drawn breath. Jen didn't want to leave this moment, she was the happiest she'd been in a long time here with her face pressed against her lover's breasts. The feel of the nipple under her cheek, a sensation that gave her more satisfaction than it ought to.

But all good things come to an end, and eventually Rena motioned for her to climb off her. She reached for some tissues on her desk and grabbed a handful, patted them against her pussy to wipe off the excess cum, then padded it against her opening. Retrieving her black satin thong from her desk drawer, she threaded her underwear back over her shoes holding the tissue in place until the elastic could hold it. Without dressing again she moved back to her chair as Jen collapsed back into her, cum still dripping from her now semi deflated cock. She was pretty sure she'd be ready to go again in a few minutes with those tits swaying in front of her. She smoothed her hair back and clipped it into a ponytail then sat at her desk as if she were still conducting a meeting, albeit with her breasts still exposed.

"So, if I were you I wouldn't worry too much about what people say about you around the office," she said, her composure back to normal. "There are some changes in the near future that might see some redundancies, a horrible business, but as you can see you are a valued employee to me, and I would very much hate to lose you." She said that with a knowing smile. "Just remember what we discussed before you make a decision about leaving the company ok."

Jen got the message. This 'meeting' was adjourned and it was time for her to leave. She retrieved her slacks and underwear and casually put them on, not wanting to look away from those beautiful breasts that seemed to defy gravity. She finished dressing and got up to leave.

"Oh and one more thing Jen. Just because myself and Rachel are good friends, doesn't mean you have to worry about me telling her the answers to her questions." She glanced down at the bulge in her slacks and gave her that beautiful warm smile again.

"Thank you Rena, I'll see you on Monday," she said, feeling a new level of confidence and assertion in her voice.

"You will. And remember Jen, my door is always open."

She smiled at that and left.

When you are out of work you will take any job and put up most things just to keep it. I do not like snobs, people who think they are a cut above everyone else and look down their noses at people they believe are of a lesser order than themselves. These people are usually shits, first class shits and the Chief Executive of the company was typical of this kind of animal but she wanted a chauffeur and I wanted a job.

"I expect you to be at work on time, I want you there when I want you, when you are taking me anywhere make sure the car is spotlessly clean, inside and out. You always refer to me as Ma'am , there will be no familiarity. You always wear the uniform during working hours, keep it clean and smart and without exception you polish your shoes until you can see your face in them, have you any questions?"

"No Ma'am ." Well as I said I needed the job.

Rena, was used to being the boss, she expected people to jump when she entered a room and usually they did.

I would pick her up about 7.30am to drive her to the office. The one pleasure I got out of it was driving her Mercedes , well apart from the other benefits and perks. I would park the Mercedes in the underground car park and after making sure it remained spotlessly clean I would go into the little office, about as big as a broom cupboard, where there was a telephone, in case the boss wanted me, there was also a kettle so I could at least make myself a cup of tea.

I need you to drive me to St. Albans, bring the car around to the front entrance. She never sat in the front seat, that would have been far beneath her and she might have felt obliged to talk to me. Sometimes when she was going abroad I would drive her to NYC, help her with her baggage and once the plane had taken off I would drive back to the garage and until she got back I could do much as I liked, and I did. If I used the Mercedes I would have to make sure I didn't over use the petrol but there was latitude. What she didn't know about was the fucking that took place on the backseat of her precious Mercedes. Chloe, the young office assistant, lost her virginity on the backseat right where she would sit, issuing orders on her phone. Chloe was to be a constant supply of cunt for me, and believe me she had a little tight one.

Another of my duties was to drive the CEO and her family to their retreat, a log cabin hidden away in the woods and leafy glades of the Adirondacks. I had the keys and it was my job to go there a few days in advance and make sure it was clean and tidy, well stocked with food and wine and chopped-wood for the log fire. Sometimes, once the log fire was blazing, I would sit on the sofa and imagine I had Rena on the white sheepskin rug stretched in front of the hearth. As I visualized Rena with her knees wide apart I would unzip my fly and flip out my rocket of a she cock. It didn't take long to fill my handkerchief with precum that I filled it with.

Today Rena called and said "pick me up at 9 a.m. please.

Almost before the Mercedes came to a halt outside the front door Rena skipped out and sat in the front seat. She was wearing a short skirt, no stockings and thigh boots just over her knees. She didn't try to hide her thighs either. She was wearing a low cut blouse with the top two buttons undone and an ample amount of cleavage on display. I had a long drive in front of me with this beautiful sexy boss of mine for company and it was going to be difficult to ignore the numerous distractions she represented.

She was a stunningly beautiful woman, stunning blue eyes and long dark hair which lapped over her shoulders and down towards her breasts which were young, smooth and firm looking, her nipples stuck out like two missiles ready to be launched from there silos. Her thighs were long white and smooth. We talked about a variety of topics on the way.

she never attempted to cover her thighs even though she was wearing a very short skirt. I kept my eyes firmly fixed on the road but it wasn't difficult to take a regular glance. Constantly she crossed and uncrossed her legs in exaggerated fashion letting her little skirt ride further up each time until her crotch was constantly on show. I knew what she was doing but she was the boss, one false move or suggestion from me and my job was gone. I have been there before with woman, they give you the come on, come and get it, then in shock horror yell, "What kind of a girl do you think I am." I'm not a lesbian.

Rena asked me to pull off the main road; saying she needed to answer the call of nature. It was dark when I turned off at the first reasonable opportunity and found the nearest country lane and stopped the Mercedes where there was a gap in the hedges. Rena got out of the car and didn't bother to disappear behind the hedges. She found an appropriate spot and in full view hitched up her skirt, crouched near the hedge, pulled her thong to one side and had a piss that seemed to last forever. I could see the stream of piss coming out of her pussy and making a little pool in the grass beneath her.
Up she got pulled her thong into place like a hammock for her cunt,

with the Mercedes headlights still on I could see she had a deliciously, shaped and protruding pubic bone. She pulled her little skirt down and straightened it out then and came back to the car and surprised me by climbing into the backseat.

" are you going to fuck me or not?" It sounded like the kind of instruction her father would give. This was a chance too good to miss. My gorgeous boss on the backseat of her Mercedes . I turned the headlights off and got into the back of the car. I unbuckled my belt and unzipped my fly and pulled my trousers and Jockeys down. Soon Rena was stretched out on the backseat, her thong was hanging on the steering wheel where I had tossed it. Her thighs were open and her head has hanging out of the car door with her long dark-hair streaming towards the ground.

I opened her thighs as wide as I could in the cramped conditions, rubbing my cockend along her sweet, little slit, spreading her young labia, I circled and massaged her clit with the hard tip of my knob-end until she was wailing for it..
"Fuck me, fuck me. Fuck me."
I slid my cock down to find the cute, little ring of her tight cunt-hole and extracted from her the longest moan I had ever heard from a woman as she took thick cock right up her sexy, little cunt.
Now I reckoned, what with the pathetically low wages I got from her, I was fully entitled to this fuck, what a delightful way to screw a boss while the company paid me

for doing it at time-and-a-half of the normal hourly rate.

There was no doubt that for Rena, feeling a woman's hard shaft inside her, was therapeutic heaven. For the first fifty or so, unhurried thrusts, I gave it to her ever so slow and deliberate, enjoying the mounting ecstasy spreading across her face and her long intakes of breath. I didn't want to just fuck her I wanted her to enjoy the feel and thick texture of my cock, to be able to dwell on each length and savour each throb, each twitch and each pulse. I guessed that she would have been fucked by many, immature and inexperienced and I wanted her know what seasoned she cock really felt like. I wanted to send such erotic feelings swirling around her brain cells. I wanted her to feel the intoxicating and rapturous feelings that a slow, length of thick cock can give a woman.

Her first orgasm was a revelation to me, it was a mixture of tormented rhapsody and spasmodic waves after which I banged her remorselessly, slamming her backwards and forwards, her head still hanging out of the car, her mouth open, gulping air until I felt hot cunt-fluid drench my pussy, I couldn't hold it and I wasn't going to pullout, I wanted to soak her hot vagina. She told me later as we drove home that it was the first-time she had ever been cummed into..she jokingly said she was on the pill and did not need the morning-after-pill. I told her to get one just in case. She had some serious sperm inside her. We laughed

She didn't stop taking about it all the way home. "Wasn't it wonderful? How was it for you? I thought it was great." I have never felt anything like it, I had an orgasm you know?"

As if I could miss it. Each orgasm she had made me feel like I was riding at a rodeo.

"It's the first time a woman has ever, you know, let it go inside me. It felt like ... really warm." She gushed. I felt it's hot rush

I got her home and took the car back to the underground car park. I took the torch from the boot of the car and looked at the backseat; there were fuck stains all over the upholstery, female cunt-fluid and thick, she cock-porridge.

Cmon inside I'm going upstairs to freshen up. I attended to my usual activities at my bosses house then proceeded upstairs.

When I got to the bedroom at the top of the big winding staircase in the luxurious sprawling mansion I found Rena laid on the bed naked, her thighs were spread wide, her knees almost at right-angles to her wide child-bearing hips. Her slit was perfect, her cunt shaved bald, the soft cheeks of her little ass merged neatly with the lips of her twat.

I stood at the bottom of the bed and started to strip off my clothes and soon stood naked with my cock hard and bending upwards. I had never seen a woman so submissive, her little ass slowly humping thin air in anticipation of the fuck she now knew was only moments away.

Rena reached between her thighs with both hands and very invitingly pulled her cunt-lips apart. I could see into her hole, she needed it fucked, I obliged.

I spent the next hour deep inside Rena's pussy; I fucked to the exotic sounds of her moans which reached a crescendo with each of her four orgasms the last of which came with her on her knees while I drilled her from behind, slapping the cheeks of her ass like riding a donkey. Finally I gave her what she really wanted most of all, a cuntful of cock-porridge.

Eight months later I was driving down the long country lane that meandered through the leafy wooded glades that was the approach to my bosses country retreat hideaway. It was a beautiful sunny Thursday morning. The boss was to spend the weekend at her country retreat and I was to get the place warmed through, stocked up with food and wine and carry out any minor maintenance that might be needed such as changing any light bulbs etc.

I fucked Rena twice more before she returned to her norm; she had become an avid cum inside me addict. Sometimes she just wanted to tease me and watch me shoot a load but mostly she wanted it where nature intended it.
I did the jobs I had been asked to do, got the log fire going and undressed before stepping into the shower. I washed away the tiredness of the long day with a rich lather of expensive soap making sure my cock received the lion's share of attention.
Stepping from the shower I rapped myself in one of The house bathrobes and got it on just as there was a loud knock on the cabin door.

CPSIA information can be obtained
at www.ICGtesting.com
Printed in the USA
LVHW010205300721
694058LV00017B/2065